Caterpillar to Butterfly

Camilla de la Bédoyère

QEB

This softcover edition first published in 2016

First published in the United States and Canada by
QEB Publishing
Part of The Quarto Group
6 Orchard, Lake Forest, CA 92630

Copyright © QEB Publishing, Inc. 2009

Library of Congress Cataloging-in-Publication Data

De la Bédoyère, Camilla.
  Caterpillar to butterfly / Camilla de la Bedoyere.
    p. cm. -- (QEB life cycles)
  Includes bibliographical references and index.
  ISBN 978-1-68297-028-7 (paperback)
  1. Butterflies--Life cycles--Juvenile literature. I. Title.
  QL544.2.D45 2010
  595.78'9156--dc22

                        2009000390

Printed and bound in China

Author Camilla de la Bédoyère
Editor Angela Royston
Designer and Picture Researcher Melissa Alaverdy

Publisher Steve Evans
Creative Director Zeta Davies
Managing Editor Amanda Askew

Words in **bold** are explained in the glossary on page 22.

Picture credits
(t=top, b=bottom, l=left, r=right, c=center, fc=front cover)

Corbis 17b Darrell Gulin, 19t Michael & Patricia Fogden, 20l Danny Lehman
Getty Images 4l Frans Lemmens, 5 Leroy Simon, 9b Kai Stiepel, 13b Kim Taylor & Jane Burton
NHPA/Photoshot 10l Kitchin & V Hurst, 10b Kitchin & V Hurst
Photolibrary Group 1b Wally Eberhart, 6b Earth Science Animals Animals, 7b Wally Eberhart, 8t Earth Science Animals, 8b Richard Day, 18–19 Don Johnston, 20–21 Radius Images
Science Photo Library 4r Pasieka, 22t Dr John Brackenbury, 23b Dr John Brackenbury
Shutterstock 1t SF photo, 2t Willem Dijkstra, 3t Markov, 6–7 Tina Rencelj, 6t SF photo, 7t Jacob Hamblin, 9t Tischenko Irina, 10t Kathy Keifer, 10c bhathaway, 11t Cathy Keifer, 11c Cathy Keifer, 11r Cathy Keifer, 11b Laurie Barr, 12–13 SF photo, 13t Jasenka Lukša, 14l Cathy Keifer, 14c Cathy Keifer, 14r, Cathy Keifer, 15t Jacob Hamblin, 15b Cathy Keifer, 16b Laurie Barr, 16l Laurie Barr, 16c Laurie Barr, 16r Laurie Barr, 17l Laurie Barr, 17r Jacob Hamblin, 22–23 Fizpok, 24t Jacob Hamblin

Contents

What is a butterfly?

A butterfly is a type of **insect**. Insects have three pairs of legs, making six legs altogether.

⇩The wings of a butterfly are covered in many tiny scales.

⇧The scales are usually patterned and colored.

4

Insect bodies are divided into three parts.
The head is the front part, and has
the eyes and mouth.

Head

Eye

Wing

Leg

Abdomen

Thorax

The **thorax** is the middle part,
where the legs and wings are attached.
The **abdomen** is the back part, where
the insect **digests** its food.

The story of a butterfly

Butterflies flutter around the plants. Female butterflies look for a place to lay their eggs.

The eggs will hatch into caterpillars. Later, the caterpillars will change into butterflies.

2

Caterpillar

1

Egg

⇧A butterfly has four stages in its life cycle.

3

The story of how an egg
grows into an adult
butterfly is called
a **life cycle**.

Pupa

4

Adult

A new life begins

In spring, a female butterfly searches for somewhere safe to lay her eggs.

She lays them under the leaves, where they are hidden from view.

Egg

⇨ Monarch butterflies lay their eggs on milkweed plants. The eggs stick to the leaves.

8

Different types of
butterfly lay their
eggs on different plants.
Peacock butterflies choose
nettles. These plants have
stinging hairs. The stings
stop animals from eating
the nettles and the eggs.

⇨Nettles are a
safe place for
peacock butterflies
to lay their eggs.

The eggs hatch

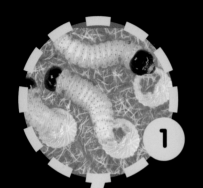

A few days later, the eggs hatch, and a tiny yellow caterpillar comes out of each one.

1

Caterpillars spend most of their time eating, so they grow quickly.

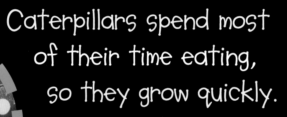

2

⇧ Monarch caterpillars become striped as they grow older.

3

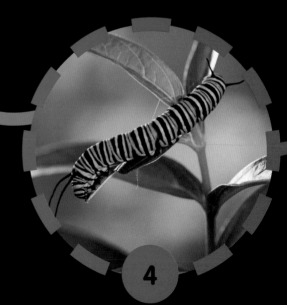

4

As a caterpillar grows, its skin becomes too tight, and splits. The caterpillar sheds its skin, revealing a new one underneath. This is called **molting**.

A caterpillar is also known as a **larva**.

⇩When a caterpillar molts, it wriggles out of its old skin.

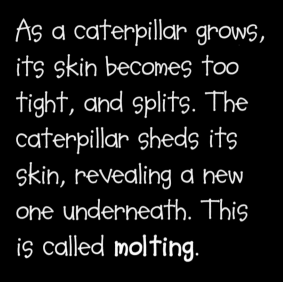

1

2

3

5

Staying alive

Caterpillars are soft and juicy—so lots of other animals want to eat them. Many caterpillars have special ways of staying alive.

Monarch caterpillars are bad to eat. Their stripes warn animals that they are **poisonous**.

⇧ The monarch caterpillar's poison comes from the milkweed plants it eats.

Many caterpillars are green, so they blend in with their surroundings.

This is called **camouflage**.

⇩A green caterpillar on a green leaf can be hard to see.

⇩Some caterpillars have sharp spines on their bodies.

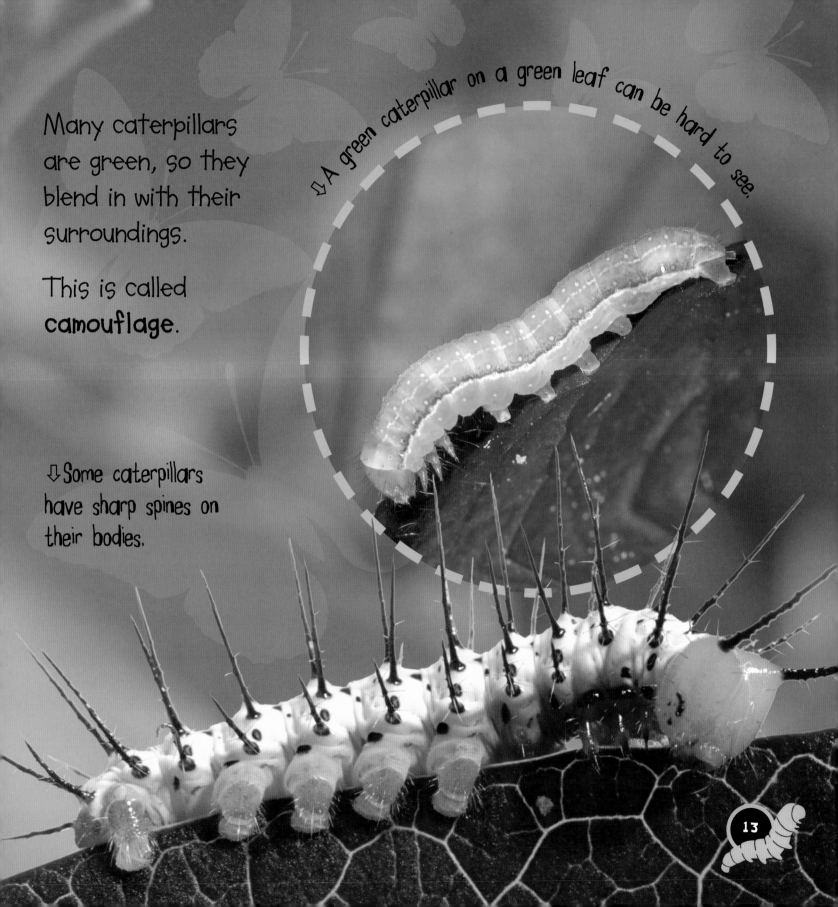

13

Making a pupa

Caterpillars grow fast. After about 14 days, a caterpillar is ready to change into a **pupa**. This is the next stage of its life cycle.

⇧ A caterpillar makes a silk thread, and uses it to hang from a leaf.

⇧ It molts for one last time. The pupa is already formed under the caterpillar's skin.

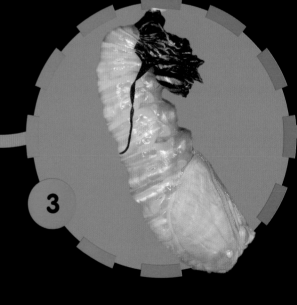

⇧ Once the skin is shed the pupa hardens.

14

A pupa is usually green or gray, so it is difficult to see on a plant. This is another example of camouflage.

5

⇦ Inside the pupa, the caterpillar gradually changes.

4

⇦ The pupa is tough on the outside to protect the insect inside.

15

A butterfly appears

After about two weeks, the pupa of the monarch butterfly becomes darker in color.

⇧ It sits on the empty pupa case.

⇧ The butterfly crawls out.

⇧ The pupa cracks open.

⇦ The orange wings of the butterfly can be seen inside.

5

⇧Then it spreads its wings so they can dry.

6

⇧It has to rest for a few hours before it can fly.

Male's dark spot

An adult butterfly does not grow any more. Male and female monarchs look similar, but males have small dark spots on their back wings.

Butterfly life

Butterflies flutter around, searching for food. They feed on sweet sugary **nectar** inside flowers.

When it is time to mate, the males follow the females. They fly around the females and push them to the ground.

18

⇨The female
lays her eggs
one at a time.

Once the butterflies
have mated, the female
lays her eggs. A new
life cycle then begins.

⇦Adults usually
live for only two
to five weeks.

A long journey

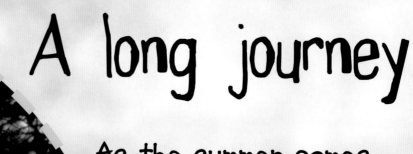

As the summer comes to an end, monarch butterflies start an amazing journey, called a **migration**.

They fly to warmer places. The journey can cover thousands of miles and takes more than two months.

⇧Millions of monarch butterflies spend the winter resting on trees.

In spring, the butterflies set off to their summer homes. On the way, they mate. Their young change into butterflies and continue the journey.

⇧The monarch butterflies wake up when warm weather arrives.

21

Glossary

Abdomen
The back part of an insect's body.

Camouflage
Patterns and colors that help an animal to hide.

Digest
When food is digested, it is changed so the body can use it to get energy. Animals need energy to live and grow.

Insect
An animal with six legs and a body divided into three parts.

Larva
Another name for caterpillar.

Life cycle
The story of how a living thing changes from birth to death and how it produces young.

Migration
A long journey made by an animal or a group of animals.

Molting
When an insect sheds, or gets rid of, its old skin.

Nectar
A sweet liquid made by flowers to attract insects to them.

Poisonous
Harmful to eat. Poison can kill living things.

Pupa
The life stage when a caterpillar changes into an adult butterfly.

Thorax
The part of an insect's body between the head and abdomen.

Notes for parents and teachers

- Look through the book and talk about the pictures.

- Safety. Teach children how to keep safe while investigating animals and their life cycles. For example, they can be shown how to recognize plants and animals that sting, or are poisonous.

- Respect for wildlife. Teach children how to observe animals and, if appropriate, handle them with care. They should observe animals in their natural environment, without disturbing them or their habitats.

- Butterfly activities. Drawing, coloring, and labeling help children to identify ways that caterpillars and adults are different. Make models together to demonstrate the stages of a butterfly's life cycle.

- Visiting a wildlife or butterfly sanctuary helps children to understand the importance of habitats. Explain the way a habitat can provide shelter and food for lots of different animals and plants.

- Be prepared for questions about human life cycles. There are plenty of books for this age group that can help you to give age-appropriate explanations.

- Talking about a child's family helps them to link life processes, such as reproduction, to their own experience. Drawing simple family trees, looking at family photo albums, and sharing family stories with grandparents are fun ways to engage young children.

24

Index